View From The
Middle of The Road

Volume II

U.S. in Us

Anthology

PRA Publishing ◊ Martinez, Georgia

ISBN 0-9727703-6-4 paperback
ISBN13 978-09727703-6-1
Library of Congress 20066929979

Cover Design by Mitchell N. Stokes

Edited by Brenda Baratto

Cover art *U.S. in Us* reproduced from an original painting by artist Toni Quest©; used with permission of the artist.

All poems featured have been used with the authors' permission.

PRA Publishing
P.O. Box 211701
Martinez, Georgia 30917
www.prapublishing.com

Printed in the United States of America

Dedication

This volume of *View* is dedicated to all the poets,
female and male. Black, white and in-between.
Christians, Jews, Islamic, Hindus and Buddhists.

Young

    And

        Old

Known and yet to be discovered.

The world needs to hear from you.

Contents

Makal Ani
A South Carolinian speaks from the heart

Lucinda Clark
A native Pennsylvanian speaks on aspects of American life

Contents

Robert Ward

A North Carolinian shares his thoughts on spirit

Toni Quest

A New Yorker trips the light fantastic

Makal Ani

- a South Carolinian speaks from the heart

Just Enough Love

There's not enough room in your body to hold all the tears you could cry

Not enough trees to make the paper to answer all the questions why

There is not enough closet space to contain the skeletons you want to hide

Ain't enough mental strength left to find a reason not to die

But there's just enough love to keep our hopes alive

And if you promise to share your love, then I promise so will I

There are not enough words in a language to express the pain inside

Not enough cheerleaders to keep you from falling behind

There's not enough respect given for you to always be polite

Aren't enough feet and fists to guarantee victory if you fight

But there is just enough love to offer you this bribe

If you promise to hold my hand, I promise to never leave your side

There's not enough room in the glass to hold the sands of healing time

Not enough depth in psychiatrics to understand what's in your mind

There's not enough experience in broken hearts to say you have any insight

There's not enough money in the world to own the joy you want to buy

But there's just enough love to open your eyes

If you're asking for contentment here is your reply

Love

Living Legend

It takes a true legend to leave behind a legacy

Many can walk the path, but a legend has clarity

Imagine having a vision and being driven when you're on your own

Where every decision for the life you're living is made by you alone

Staying focused on a goal until the destination is reached

Seeing nothing but success when staring at defeat

When it's finally done and you're at the mountain's peak

You want to celebrate, but it feels so incomplete

There's no satisfaction in knowing the way to freedom

When your fellow men are captive because no one will lead them

Martin Luther King led peaceful demonstrations

Malcolm X's words stirred the entire nation

W.E.B. Du Bois said to get an education

Booker T. Washington said a trade is true emancipation

Harriet Tubman told the slaves, "We can leave at sunset."

Christ says, "If you come I will gladly accept"

A legend isn't created when a story is told or written

Acts of love and courage are done by the living

Fame and acknowledgement are given to a name

The real reward is accomplishing the dream

Living by faith is a hard thing to do

So if you master this art, then the legend is you

In Your Eyes

In your eyes I see the sadness a smile can't hide

The reminiscence of a broken heart when those three words lied

In your eyes I see the rain and dark storm clouds

Growing into an emotional hurricane until you express it out loud

In your eyes I see the fear of never being understood

Thinking if you removed your mask no one would ever look

In your eyes I see the deep longing to be touched and kissed

But questioning will it start something real or simply be left at this

In your eyes I see the little girl you tried to leave behind

You put her on punishment but she won't stay in a corner of your mind

In your eyes I see that precious innocence you want to lose

But you're waiting on that one man worth breaking the rules

In your eyes I see the confusion of being pulled in every direction

Any many miny moing to receive a curse or a blessing

In your eyes I see the hurt you feel for someone else

Vowing in the mirror to never go through this yourself

In your eyes you show me everything I wanted to see

A perfect woman looking for love to erase her insecurities

A Dance Without Romance

I look at her and it's easy to tell

She's being taken care of, and he's doing it well

Her hair is long and smooth. It flows like satin

Her beauty is perfection, as if God took time to practice

Skin ever so soft, yet her body is so tight and firm

Her existence is simple proof that prayers do get answered

Then I look again, and I see a silent yearning

An unfulfilled desire has her body burning

She's locked in a stable being loved and groomed

But boredom is fueling her to bust out the room

Tired of being a trophy showcased for the world to see

She's dying to have a moment to just run free

Life would be perfect if he enjoyed simple things

But his world is making money and his computer screens

So now, here she is with a little time to kill

But everyone who approaches is ready to kneel

I understand the need she wants to have met

She wants a night of distorted memories she could almost
forget

The puzzle of her life is just about complete

All she really wants is to enjoy a dance with me

When She Cries

When she cries

my fast-paced world

slows to an

unrushed moment

When she sheds a tear

my Sunday drive

hurries to a

cross-town dash

When her eyes water

my sun shiny day

darkens to a

cold stormy night

When she boo hoos

my egotistical boast

deflates to a

saddened question "why"?

When she weeps

my raised fists of triumph

open to two

arms of consolation

When she breaks down

my life-threatening problem

diminishes to an

insignificant after thought

When she chokes up

my hard chiseled body

softens to a

yielding pillow of comforting

When her eyes overflow

my joyous yells of "YES"

lower to

somber whispers of "I know"

When her pain is expressed

my prayer of gratitude

is accompanied with

a supplication for her relief

When she cries

I have to cry too.

How can I

be happy alone?

Lustful Haikus

A true sign of lust
is feeling love at first sight.
To love you must know.

Love: a decision,
not an uncontrolled impulse.
Who falls on purpose?

What is it about
the beautiful scenery
that makes us clumsy?

Blinded by our sight,
reality is unseen.
Hearts are handicapped.

Lust is a season
Love endures through all seasons
Time tells the story

Flurries of snow dance
to passion's song in my mind.
My heat makes it melt.

What Do We Want?

So many wars to fight and battles to win
To keep history from repeating again
But what part of the past are we trying to avoid
Do we know what we're saying or just making noise
History isn't repeating. The record is skipping
We're stuck in this rut and time is still ticking
Decades have passed as we demand equality
Marching on a treadmill and it's appalling to me
With every great chance to make our stand
We fall because of mistakes made by the revered man
It's sad, but I don't think we know why we fight anymore
What's messed-up is it's not the same enemy as it was before
In the jungle of society looking for white oppressors
Getting shot in the back by those who protect us
The enemy doesn't have blond hair and blue eyes
He looks just like us and don't act surprised
We've been fighting ourselves and blaming another race
When we sold ourselves into slavery in the first place
Even as slaves there was a great divide
Field niggers picking cotton and house niggers inside
When we finally got our freedom we wanted integration
Years down the road and here comes The Nation
Telling us the answer is actually segregation
But that's expected when they recruit from incarceration
Do we want education or do we want a trade?
Do we want to keep a job or know how to get paid?
Until we come together and define our need
We will always be our own worst enemy
It's been said there will be war until the end of time
So I don't seek a resolution, just a peace of mind

Political Leader?

Looking to a
leader who has
conflicts of interest
The inevitable
undoing of
our plight
Any great
captain goes down
with the ship
but nowadays
the crew is more
dedicated to
the cause
The leader
makes sure he's
around to fight
Pause
A political field
for a social war?
Change the channel
Heard these
promises before
A strong black
man with black
people at his back
understands he's
not a leader
He's a shield
during attacks
No great leader
looks in the
mirror and sees
a great man
He sees his
family at his
side holding his
hand
With this
picture in his
mind he's
determined to
stand
It will take
a mighty blow
to keep him
down because
where there's
a goal and
there's a plan
there's the strength
to rise
again and again
That's why leaders
should be in
the homes not
just to be
the man but to
pass the torch on
It takes an
intimate love
to be ready
to die for
a cause
When the wife
says "baby"
and the kids
say "daddy"
a man is above
political laws
Wait 'til
he's dead
before you applaud

Unfounded Truths

Can't take the world personal

Happiness is comical

Had to learn to be obstinate

So my future won't be a duplicate

I wish I could talk to the press

about living in destituteness

Confess my contempt for the U.S.

Only thing in this land for me is cess

Still I travel on an endless journey

to reach the status of M.D.s and attorneys

Not professional just monetarily

The thought of being poor forever is scaring me

Have to escape the footsteps of the past

My parents didn't leave any rope to grab

All they left me is a rising tab

Might be mad but all I can do is laugh

I understand things are different than they were

Every new year brings a different hurt

White folks have hidden smirk

Have to have jewelry just to flirt

The idea of a virgin is absurd

And it's a devil's fest in the church

Where is the world heading to?

What does the government have to prove?

Who's representing these shoes?

How was I born just to lose?

I'm so tired of being lost and confused

One side of the story on the news

All their rich and all our dead

All their proud and all our scared

All their blessings and honorable mentions

All our crimes and poverty quenchings

Struggling of welfare and social systems

So much to say but no one to listen

Every attempt for justice fails

Especially for those dangerous black males

Too much baggage to go anywhere

Way too strong for the game to be fair

Too many thugs to represent

To ever be elected president and barely mayor

Reduced to belief in soothsayers

Because it seems God doesn't answer prayers

I'm stuck in the midst of the devil's lair

And he's a bitch with a blunt playing in my hair

Guess he knows that's my only weakness

Women and weed are how I get blessed

I Had A Dream

I had a dream the world understood
the system God had in place
and that if we simply followed the plan
we wouldn't have the problems we face

I had a dream of the racial barriers
that need to be broken down
so we can love each other for who we are
and not because our skin is white or brown

I had a dream that the whole world
understood the evil of stereotypes
and knew that the book color
could not tell the story inside

I had a dream respect was given innately
and not demanded by force
so that when we wronged any man
our conscience made us remorse

I had a dream society wasn't so greedy
letting money dictate every move
but viewed the much bigger picture
the more we gain, the more we really lose

I had a dream, money and looks weren't the issues
when it came to finding true love
but values and being compatible
is all we were in search of

I had a dream we stopped double standards
idolizing the player and degrading the hoe
rather, teaching the young fornication is wrong
because responsibility is a word they don't know

I had a dream that men realized
the importance of their presence
not dropping in every now and then
but a positive model from birth through adolescence

I had a dream that every man
viewed love and sex as a beautiful thing
and understood if it's worth enjoying
it's worth commitment with a ring

I had a dream that when a man said "I do"
he really meant it from his heart
and if he was given the role of husband and father
he was diligent and faithful in playing the part

I had a dream that women reared the girls
to be women in the house
to cook, clean, be loving and supportive
and be desirable as a life long spouse

I had a dream that one day
we could all live in a perfect world
where a female wasn't abused
because she had the strength of a girl

I had a dream of a glorious day
when every woman could love and respect herself
and no man could treat her like trash
because she defined her own wealth

I had a dream of the years of inequality
and how it caused our women to be so feisty
and I saw a day when all men and women
could communicate about anything politely

I had a beautiful dream
of a fantasy that could become real
but it would take devotion to the plan
for God's values to be instilled

That's What I Thought

Time is un-centered and unjustified; a paper written with no symmetry, a decision made with no consulting, an ever-present entity in every physical equation. Can you grade the paper poorly, or just call it a perfect poem? Can you demand a retrial, or just live with the ruling? Can you ignore how long it takes, or just continue to calculate?

Time is immeasurable and unbalanced; a tool used by God, a birthday unseen in some years, an ever-running line from in the beginning to eternity.

Can you ask God why, or just appreciate His choice? Can you blame the stars, or just make amends to the calendar? Can you bend the line, or just exist between your points?

Ever wonder why time is called Father and earth is called Mother? Are we the offspring of their union? Is Father Time the entity God was talking to when He said, "Let us"? If we were formed in the image of Time and God, and both are ageless, does age really matter? What is age? What is a natural certainty that occurs at a specific age? How long had Adam lived before God realized he needed a companion? After He realized it, how many conversations did He have with Time before he acted? If we realize a need for change, when should we start the process? That's what I thought.

Lucinda Clark

- a native Pennsylvanian speaks on aspects of American life

A Times Table Tale

Time
Marches on
Heals all
Tells all

Time is
Watched
Marked
Measured

Time
Goes on
Goes too slow
Goes too fast

Times are
Good
Bad
Remembered
Forgotten

Time is

Used wisely
Wasted
Managed

Time to

Laugh
Cry
Be happy
Be sad
Take a stand

One can have time
Robbed
Sacrificed
Stolen

Time is special
We had the time of our lives
The time we spent was special
I am glad
I took the time

Time marks occasions
Holiday time
Work time
Time to grieve
Time to rest
Time for family
Time for friends

Time is questioned

Where did it go?
What time is it?
Will I have enough of it?

And Finally

Time will
Explain why things that have come to pass
Mark a beginning or an ending

Why do we put so much emphasis on time?
Because we do not know how much we truly have

Until

It is gone
Time is God given
To mark it
Measure it
Waste it
Worry about it
Give it away
Rejoice in it
Reflect on it
Sell it to the highest bidder
Or give it to a child
Are all choices we are given
How will you use your time today?

A Voice From The Future

You fear me
Because I shatter on sight
The myths you hold near and dear.
The beliefs you cling to so desperately
With all your heart.

You must hear me.
 The threat in your mind is not real
 The truth that you cling to
 Stands like a house of straw
 Ready to be toppled by the forceful winds of reality.

Don't scare me
With your uncivilized talk
Of how you are right
And I am wrong

Just prepare me
For my place in the world
Will be secured.

My destiny
Found in your ability
To change with the times.

To embrace the notion
That belief's like
One's mind
Can be revised, edited or just changed.

Woman On Power Tools

Woman works in her garden
Cultivating the soil gently
By hand
While all around her
Her fellow gardeners (men)
Work with power tools

Mowing
Sawing
Tilling
Blowing
Such noise!

One day the woman gets a lesson
A simple one
How to turn a power tool on

She blows leaves
The vibrations from the tool are strong

She learns to saw limbs
That would take years to fall
They now succumb in minutes

She learns to use a tiller
Planting bulbs and flowers, that once took weeks
Now takes hours.

The woman gardener has joined the men's club
She appreciates the time saved
With power tools.

Baseball

In the stands,
Sit the fans,
Waiting for the game to begin.

Out come the players.
Team colors displaying
Waving and working the crowd.

The umpires
Take off their glasses
In preparation
Of calling each play

The coaches pace
Back and Forth
Wondering
Will we get creamed today?

The first batter steps up
"Strike one!" Yells the ump
The batter prepares again to swing away.
"Strike two!" Motions the ump.
The batter now tenses up.
"Strikeeee Three, You're out!"
The crowd hears the ump say
As the batter's hope and bat fall away.

Ode to Moms Everywhere

Love is the feeling
That beats in the heart
Of every chest.
It is reserved for the woman
That we acknowledge today
For giving her best

This love begins for us before we are born
It grows and takes root
Even after she passes on.

For as youngsters
It was mom who seldom failed
As
Protector,
Teacher,
Confidante, (fendo)
Nag.
And it is in these memories we realize.
We had love in the bag.

As teens
It was mom who cheered us to our best
Who cried inside, when we were sad
Who encouraged us, when we were unsure of talents
Who provided guidance and direction
Whenever we found ourselves off balance.

As adults
With families of our own to raise.
Mom's lessons, given directly
By example and with praise
Now pass to the next generation
Becoming our lessons
As we struggle as parents
In our child-rearing days.

For all the days of conflict
Between what mom knows and we know as best.
It is on this day, Mother's Day
All conflicts get a rest.

For unconditional love is the rarest of things
Can dads give it?
Sure, that's the other holiday.

For the love that is shared between a mother and her child
Even if you don't understand it
Wait a little while.

For it grows more enduring with each passing day
And throughout life's ups and downs
Never, ever goes away.

Bad News and Telephones

Good news never comes by phone in the middle of the night

It comes in the bright morning hours
It comes in the hours between 9 and 5
Just in time to celebrate!
Just in time to tell a friend.

Heart wrenching bad news seems to pay its visit in late night hours

Or

Early, early in the morning, when the mind and body lay sleeping

It is hard to comprehend the news once it is received.
Sleep is lost for what seems like forever.

The mind wrestles with the essence of the tragedy.
The mind says this is but a bad dream.

Then dawn arrives.
And with it,
Song birds
Coffee and
Morning rituals

The night call seems like a far off occurrence.
Until.......
The telephone rings again
and preparations must begin.

Something Lost

We strive to move into the mainstream

We educate

Placate

Assimilate

As we strive to move into the mainstream

We learn to

Dress well

Speak well

Write well

And we do well

As we strive to move into the mainstream

We buy homes in areas that

A few decades ago would not have us.

We take on memberships in the right clubs

We send our children to schools

Where some of the parents believe

our presence brings down the quality of the education

As we strive to move into the mainstream

We never assess the "price" to be paid

To be there.

Only struggle with the "cost" to stay.

When we arrive in the mainstream

The culture left behind looks different

The explanations given for our culture's plight sound different

The hopelessness and helplessness seems unreal

Once settled in the mainstream
Slights which once were sure to be intentional
Take on a new orientation
The labels we wear identify our culture
They are worn like a badge of courage.

The ease with which we dismiss injustices becomes a
A comfortable fit.
The empty chatter at social gathers becomes less forced.

Oh yes, we have arrived
In the mainstream
Tired from the swim against mighty currents
Stronger from rolling the boulder uphill.

Every now and again

We question, is it worth it.
If we remain true to our forefathers.
You can bet it is

If we look at our children
Who now scoff
Whenever we mention the struggle
Who become fearful when we travel into the "hood"
Who insist the times have changed.

We find that the move into mainstream
Brings money, comfort and some pain
Because to thrive
There must be a shedding of original culture
The loss of language, history and name.
We gain facelessness in the crowd
Static indifference to our old brother's pain

But we have the American Dream
A dream that did originally include us
It is a dream we say we understand
How so, when the molders and shapers
of the dream
were not brown, copper or tan.

Why

Why have the skies opened up
and sent this rain?
With a sky so ominous, menacing and gray.

What is that loud clamp of thunder in the distance?
As I move closer
I recognize it as the wail of sorrows.

Sorrow from many hearts,
Broken
Aching
Ripped from wounded chests.

Where is the shelter
for which I can rest?

Rest from the lack of sleep.
The same old thoughts,
that what has happened was somehow for the best.

The plan.
I dare not question

The signs.
I cannot ignore

Our God is with us.

Watching

Waiting

Judging

Is free will the answer?

Oh faith you must not flee,

because the sun is right above me.

I must now look a little harder.

For it is with faith

I will be allowed to see

To The People I Leave Behind

Sing no more sad songs for me
For my time in this realm has passed.

My spirit now soars
High - expanding beyond the clouds
Wider and farther than the deepest blue sea
So big. Much bigger than the old physical me.

You mourn what you knew – my former self
Just think
My soul is transformed
I am now something else.

Shed a tear
Shed many
As long as it is done
In celebration, rejoicing, over my victory won.

For my Lord has called
Brought me home
Changed me.

We will meet again
although I cannot say when
it is my hope you will recognize the new me.

For I may be the subtle, soothing sound of a rainy day
Or a star shining brightly in a clear evening sky
Or one of the elements of a sunset or a moving sunrise.

Know too
That you cannot be with me
For there are more great things for you, in this realm
 More that has to be done

The final message I wish to leave with thee
Is the realization, that in my old life
 I tried to be
Worthy of every single tear
That you now shed for me.

Hold me in your heart
Remember me well
For I too will miss you terribly
Yet,
Must still bid you farewell.

Anguish

If there is such a thing as grief beyond imaging
I have felt it.

If there is such a thing as despair beyond reckoning
I have seen it.

If there is such a thing as ongoing tragedy
With no end in sight
I have been a witness.

If there is such a thing as time heals all wounds
I now pray for it.

Robert Ward

- a North Carolinian shares his thoughts on spirit

Strangers On The Road

An old man journeyed the Whreymire Road
before a storm one night;
He sought a place to rest his head
and wait for morning's light.

He stopped to camp just off the road
and sat before his fire;
To eat and rest, perhaps to sleep;
but wrote 'til he grew tired.

He journaled all his travels
about his search for honest men;
And hoped that in his tireless search,
he'd find the truth within.

Then from the trees a Stranger came,
to the edge of the campfire light.
And bade the man, "May I join you there;
to share the lonely night?"

A chilling wind from nowhere came,
encircling the man,
He shook the chill from 'round him off;
and simply nodded his head.

I will not bid you welcome,
so you cannot choose to stay.
For I will on my way alone,
come nigh the break of day.

The Stranger cast a sickening smile
and sat before the fire,
he sat and stared as the old man wrote,
for hour upon hour.

Another Stranger approached the camp,
claiming kinship to the other.
And asked to join them for the night
while waiting for another.

The old man nodded toward a space
beside the other man.
Two dark visitors in the night
awaiting another of their brand.

Blood ran from the second stranger's eyes,
his voice a silent hiss.
He asked the old man about his life
and how he had come to this.

The man said "I will not answer you,
nor will I choose to sleep.
For on this dark and lonely road,
my counsel will I keep."

"We know what lies on the road ahead"
they said to the rising wind.
And stared as one into the old man's eyes,
"We know what lies within."

They cackled loud, a flash of light,
a rise of storm and rain.
But round the camp, the ground stayed dry
as the dust when he first came.

The thump of heavy heartbeats
rang in rhythm with the thunder,
the very earth itself was shaken
as something came from under.

From down the road, a wagon came,
its axles wreathed in flame.
A load of bones and corpses shook,
all smoking as it came.

Its driver stopped before the camp,
black horses without eyes.
And asked if he could join them
'til the light has touched the skies.

His cloak was black, rank and torn;
his face all leathern skin.
He stepped down from the wagon and said,
"Won't you invite me in?"

I will not bid you welcome,
so you cannot choose to stay.
For I will on my way alone,
come nigh the break of day.

I travel to my mother's house,
just o'er the northern hill;
For word has come to me of how
she has grown gravely ill.

I've learned much in my travels
and I come to bring her aid,
lest she lose herself in circumstance,
and leave this life, he said.

We also journey to this place,
to see your lonely mother;
and keep her company one last time,
since she has had no other.

The aid you bring is much too little;
moreover, much too late.
She'll take her fall to darkness,
for we three now hold her fate.

"I think not" said the old man,
"You'll not go there this night."
I came this way because of you,
to set all things to right.

"What chance have you?" hissed the former two,
"You've one foot in the grave!"
"No warrior's countenance comes from you,
what power do you have?"

The old man reached into his sack,
and pulled a battered book;
that blazed with light so brilliant,
that the Strangers could not look.

"What sorcery is this the Hissers screamed,
the Driver ran for cover.
"I've entertained you much too long", he said.
"This conversation is over."

In thundering and flames of fire,
the Strangers disappear.
and left the old man standing
as he wiped a single tear.

The old man left his camp
and journeyed over the hill to home,
and came to find his mother
who was ill, so very much alone.

She forgave him for her lonely days
as he read to her from the book;
that earlier drove the strangers off
with just a single look.

"How fared you with them?" she had asked.
They did not come this way,
What stopped them on their journey here
before the break of day.

"I asked God for forgiveness
and the way to set you free."
All He gave me was his Word
and said bring it back with me.

I did not know it's Power
'til this dark and lonely night,
when I saw Fear, Death and
Damnation put to flight.

They left me and they couldn't take you,
the Lord's Word is strong,
against Forgiveness, Faith and Hope,
they did not last for long.

His mother safe, his travels through,
he signed his final page.
And learned his greatest lesson
at an unexpected age.

This road of life we travel,
is filled with fears and dread,
but we can conquer all of them
if we use faith instead.

So on your dark road journey
when the Strangers come to call,
just open the Book of Faith and Hope,
For God's Word conquers all.

Mulberry Dreams

I dream a story of sunshine past
and summers long ago,
Of sandy hills and fields of green
only little boys can know.

A bluer sky you'll never see
the night sky split asunder,
I ride on memories backward
amid summer storms and thunder.

Red clay fields and dodge ball skills
oak trees as tall as heaven,
and fried chicken Sunday afternoons
with music 'til eleven.

Through mulberried streets of Jamestown
my alley kingdoms reigned,
with comic books and cowboys
a boy's mind runs again.

And dreams of a man I'll soon become
of distant feats undone,
Down through the years I still remain
my beloved father's son.

To the courageous couple that bore the children
that played beneath the tree,
I wander back over the fence once more
and bend a grateful knee.

And thank the Lord for times retold
through a little boy's memory,
and the parents, sister, friends and more
That all come back to me.

The hair has grayed, no fields remain
my running days no more,
I ride on toward the sunset
but my memories are still sure.

Of 300 Mulberry, always home
only now in memory,
I live this life a story told
That I read secretly.

And wonder how God made me
as one page upon another,
I start and end my journey
as my only sister's 'brother.'

Victory of The Spirit

Through seven doors - and five unseen,

the hidden line that lies between;

the Spirit pure, the Body and Mind;

the Vessel's cure, the Word divine.

The Hidden Man, more precious than gold,

through pages in stages, life's story is told;

the Riddle's answer lies - you see,

In the realignment of the Three.

The Hidden Man must grow and lead;

each motivation, thought and deed.

Spirit to Mind to Body unite,

Forever meditating on the Right.

Unlearn, enlighten, evaluate;

Which one is leading will determine your fate.

The Spirit must lead, its root divine

more superior in purpose, than body or mind.

The Battleground becomes the Mind

for as you think - you do.

So guard well the entrance to your Heart.

Its wellspring is life to you.

For in your heart is what your Mind believes

What you believe and speak; your Faith achieves.

We unleash our Powers we cannot see;

Speaking things that be not - as though they be.

When we learn to believe,
in the things invisible;
We will see manifested,
what we thought impossible.

As Gods untrained, our weapons are words,
From the mind of the Father of Light;
Belief in His words, is our sure salvation,
As we fight our earthly fight.

For it is surely warfare,
and our lives are at stake;
As the appointed Time draws near.
Be aware of the Enemy, or your life he will take;
The weapon he uses is Fear.

The most destructive weapons the enemy has
in his deceitful arsenal from Hell.
Are the lies and fears and unbelief,
We bring to the battlefield ourselves.

So become invincible in this earthly life,
and keep the Enemy from you.
Meditate on the Word, Speak the Word,
And as you're guided - Do.

Willow's Song

Do willows dream an endless sleep,
of earthly woes, and why they weep?
Their melancholy spirits steep,
in the urn of heaven's tears.

For willow's ear, the song is strained,
the earth's impassioned soul's refrain;
whose bark becomes a cure for pain,
a treasure through the years.

Wisdom she cries in the silent wind,
and nurtures virtue deep within;
her earthly mother underpins,
the rhyming in the snow.

This song that only trees can hear,
this instrument strung without an ear;
Bids winter's dream to disappear,
the way that seasons go.

In blooming elegance, April's dream,
the melancholy dream it seems;
in pastures bound in blossom leans,
is reborn from the sleep.

With clouds and thunder, storm's embrace,
a seedling springs with nature's grace;
a child is born to fill the place,
no sorrowful song could keep.

As summer's stormy tumults cease,
with spearhead leaves a dream release,
Oak's mournful sister sighs in peace,
life's dance beneath the shade.

A canopy of weeping eyes
sways in the breeze, but realize;
that seasons turn to finalize,
the sonnet she has made.

So willow dreams of songs untold,
that drown the darkness of the cold;
of life reborn in days of olde,
and things that soon must be.

Life's cycles mark the march of time,
in tears marked in the willow vine;
her path to God the same as mine,
a weeping willow tree.

The Hand

In a world filled with the filth of
prejudice, injustice, inequality,
war, blood and death,

I rise.

From the bleakness of poverty
and the darkness of despair,
my spirit screams against the chains of indifference;
the ignorance and complacency of inaction.

The predators of the streets,
the opportunists, the profiteers,
the arrogant rich, the prideful and perverse.
I am your nightmare given form,
your dread given the shape of Night.

You stand on the neck of all Mankind,
a stranglehold you will not release without a fight.
So be it. The choice is made.

I rise.

For the humble, the victimized,
the blood of the innocent,
and the justice long denied them,
May Heaven forgive me,

I rise.

I am the Darkness. The Vengeance.

the Harvest of your Evil seeds.

Let Hell and all who worship it, beware.

I rise.

May Heaven have mercy, for I will not.

Watch the wall.

The writing begins.

I rise.

Toni Quest

- a New Yorker trips the light fantastic

Chocolate

Why is chocolate so bad?
They call it a goody
And it clings to my booty

Because it loves me
For who I am

So why is chocolate so bad?
It tastes really good
Elevates my mood
Even replaces real food, sometimes

Melts and slides over my tongue
Ahh , it really is so much fun

Some say I'm pathetic
Luckily I'm not diabetic
Surely you're empathetic
This is not an epidemic

It's a trend
To savor with a friend
Is that really so bad?

So why is it wrong to touch this stuff?
When it makes me smile so nicely,
And the smell of it always excites me
Ooo, so very enticing

Rich,
Smooth,
Dark,
Sweet,
Seductive
This is my favorite thing
Chocolate.

Bum Deal

You painted your portrait

It was so true to life

Rare and refined

I made my grant

A good offer

Me.

Then you spent me.

I Love It When

I love it when you touch me nice,

Not just once or twice,

But all the times you touch me nice.

I love it.

I love it when you smile at me:

It captures me

Sincerely

I love it when you kiss me long

I feel your love so clearly

I love it.

Fly

Fly

I want to fly,

Break out of these shackles that impede me

And FLY;

Glide high,

With strength and ease,

Be free,

Be swift,

Fly high;

Touch the sky,

Slide through the clouds

Wave at the sun

Dance with the stars

Sing with the moon

Soar High

Fly

Posing With No Clothes

Posing with no clothes

Almost everything shows,

From my noses to my toes

So let me state

Before it's too late,

I still look great,

Because the shutter exposes

Much more than my poses

Rather my passion

Which, is no longer rationed

So turning 50

Is really quite nifty

So lucky to postpone

The boob and face lifty

www.ingramcontent.com/pod-product-compliance
Lightning Source LLC
Chambersburg PA
CBHW061843040426
42447CB00012B/3107